Copyright © 2025 by Jonathan P. Saunders

All rights reserved.

No part of this publication may be reproduced, stored in a retrieval system, or transmitted in any form or by any means—electronic, mechanical, photocopy, recording, or otherwise—without the prior written permission of the publisher, except for brief quotations used in reviews or scholarly works.

Immigration: The Line We Draw

First Edition

ISBN: 979-8-9929790-5-3

Published by Saunders Consigliere PLLC

Printed in the United States of America

Library of Congress Control Number: Pending

The views expressed in this book are those of the author and do not necessarily reflect the official policy or position of any government, organization, or entity. While every effort has been made to ensure accuracy, the author and publisher assume no responsibility for errors or omissions.

Interior design and formatting by Saunders Consigliere PLLC

Immigration: The Line We Draw

How Nations Choose Who Belongs—and Who Doesn't

Jonathan P. Saunders

Saunders Consigliere PLLC

Dallas, Texas

Table of Contents

- **Introduction** – P. 1
- **Chapter 1** – Why People Move: The Forces Behind Modern Migration – P. 4
- **Chapter 2** – Host Nations Under Pressure: The Quiet Frontlines of Migration – P. 11
- **Chapter 3** – Fortress Europe: The Politics of Deterrence and Denial – P. 16
- **Chapter 4** – The Asian Paradox: Dependency Without Acceptance – P. 21
- **Chapter 5** – The China Exception: Control Without Dependence – Migration, Identity, and Power in a Nation Built to Keep Its Borders Closed – P. 27
- **Chapter 6** – Myths, Memes, and Morality: The War Over Migration Narratives – P 33
- **Chapter 7** – Immigration and National Identity: Who Gets to Belong – P. 38
- **Chapter 8** – The Business of Borders: Profit, Power, and the Industry of Exclusion – P. 42
- **Chapter 9** – Selective Compassion: Who We Help, Who We Don't, and Why – P.47
- **Chapter 10** – America in Context: Myths, Hypocrisy, and the Manufactured Crisis – P. 52
- **Chapter 11** – The Global Tide: Migration in the 21st Century – P. 56
- **Chapter 12** – A Moral Reckoning: Who We Are When the Borders Close – P. 60
- **Chapter 13** – The Future in Motion: Migration in a Shifting World – P. 65
- **Conclusion** – Lines We Draw, Futures We Choose – P. 69

Introduction – Immigration: Not Just America's Story

In the minds of many Americans, immigration is seen as a uniquely American dilemma. It unfolds on our southern border, in our cities and detention centers, in presidential debates and prime-time headlines. It is framed as an "issue"—not a human reality, but a political device, used to stir fear or signal compassion. The narrative suggests that the world is desperate to come here, and only here. That America alone is the gravitational center of global migration.

We are not. And we never were.

Migration is not uniquely American. It is not even uniquely modern. Since the beginning of recorded history, people have crossed borders, deserts, mountains, and seas—for food, for family, for safety, for opportunity, for survival. What has changed in the 21st century is not the instinct to move, but the scale, speed, visibility, and volatility of that movement. Migration today is a defining challenge of the global era—shared by rich and poor countries alike, by democracies and dictatorships, by cities and states and supranational blocs.

This book is an invitation—and a provocation—to see that shared reality clearly.

We will trace the global movement of human beings—from rural to urban, south to north, east to west—and the forces that drive, distort, and deny that movement: war, climate change, economic inequality, demographic collapse, nationalism, and the legacy of empire. We will examine not just the migrants themselves, but the host countries that absorb, exploit, reject, or transform them. And we will explore how immigration has been weaponized politically in countries as different as Hungary and Honduras, India and Israel, the United Kingdom and the United States.

Here's what you won't find in this book:

- Simplistic binaries of "good immigrants" vs. "bad immigrants"
- Lazy debates about "open borders" versus "national sovereignty"
- A narrow, U.S.-only perspective filtered through partisan lenses

Instead, you'll find a cold, clear reckoning with the global migration system we've built, a system that allows capital to move freely while trapping people behind lines drawn by race, power, politics, and fear. Immigration is not just a policy debate. It is a moral x-ray. It shows who gets to move, who gets to stay, and who gets to belong. It reveals not just our laws, but our values.

To be blunt:

If you think immigration is simply about "illegal crossings," you are not seeing the world as it is.

If you think the United States faces an "unprecedented crisis," you haven't looked at Lebanon, or Colombia, or Bangladesh.

If you think you understand who "deserves" citizenship, you may not realize how arbitrary the rules are—and who gets to write them.

And if you think immigrants are the problem, you've been handed a scapegoat instead of the truth.

Yes, some of the most dangerous voices are those who know better but choose to lie—because fear is more useful than fact, and truth doesn't fit on a bumper sticker. But complicity also comes from silence, from indifference, from the failure to ask deeper questions.

This book demands more. From the narrative. From the public. From the reader.

Because in the years ahead, migration will not be a footnote. It will be one of the forces reshaping global politics, economics, and identity. It will expose the contradictions between law and morality, between sovereignty and humanity, between security and justice.

If we fail to understand this moment globally, we will fail to navigate it justly.

Before we debate where migrants go, we must understand why they leave.

Migration begins not at the border—but at the breakdown. Of safety. Of opportunity. Of home.

That is where this journey begins.

Chapter 1 – Why People Move: The Forces Behind Modern Migration

In popular memory, migration is often told as a story of hope. A family boards a ship in search of freedom. A worker leaves his village to send money home. A woman crosses a border to escape oppression and rebuild her life. These stories are not false—but they are incomplete. They tell us about the courage of individuals, not the conditions that compel them.

To understand modern migration, we must let go of the idea that movement is always a choice. Today, more often than not, migration is coerced—driven by collapsing systems, climate disruption, political violence, and a global economy that profits from stillness even as it depends on movement.

This chapter does not ask, "Why do they come?" It asks, "What is breaking in the world that pushes people to leave?" The answers do not begin at the border. They begin in bombed-out cities, in parched farmland, in cartel-controlled neighborhoods, and in trade systems that treat labor as extractive fuel, not as life.

The Myth of the Voluntary Migrant

For generations, Western societies told a simple story: the brave immigrant drawn to freedom and opportunity. In the U.S., this narrative is carved into Ellis Island, repeated in textbooks, and echoed in campaign speeches. It is tidy. Familiar. But in the 21st century, it is no longer true.

Most global migration today is not aspirational. It is urgent. Strategic. Desperate.

Over 280 million people currently live outside their country of birth. Of these, more than 110 million are forcibly displaced: refugees, asylum seekers, internally displaced persons. These are not adventurers—they are survivors. They did not migrate for a better life. They migrated to stay alive.

When media report "waves" or "surges" of migrants, what we are witnessing is not a border failure. It is the fallout of systems that failed long before the border: failures of peace, governance, climate, and economic justice.

Collapse Is the Great Mover

Syria's civil war turned cities like Aleppo into ruins. Over 13 million Syrians—more than half the pre-war population—have been displaced. Some fled to Jordan or Turkey. Others drowned in the Mediterranean. A few made it to Europe. Most remain in limbo.

Collapse is not unique to Syria. It defines modern Afghanistan, South Sudan, Myanmar, Venezuela—countries where law has disintegrated and daily life is ruled by fear.

In Central America, collapse wears a different face: gangs. In El Salvador and Honduras, cartels extort, conscript, rape, and kill with impunity. Whole communities are governed by threat. Mothers flee not toward dreams, but away from nightmares.

These are not economic migrants. They are refugees in all but name. Their displacement is not caused by random poverty—but by systems of violence—often underwritten by global arms sales, narcotics demand, and Cold War legacies.

Migration begins when societies break. We just notice it when the broken arrive at our borders.

The Climate Is Coming

By mid-century, climate change could become the single largest driver of migration worldwide. It is not a distant threat—it is already reshaping lives.

In Africa's Sahel, desertification destroys farmland and incites deadly clashes over water and grazing rights. In Bangladesh, rising seas swallow villages. In the Pacific, islands like Tuvalu and Kiribati prepare for their own extinction.

The World Bank projects up to 143 million internal climate migrants by 2050 in just three regions: Latin America, Sub-Saharan Africa, and South Asia. That doesn't even count cross-border displacement—often undocumented and invisible.

And it is not only the Global South. In the United States, hurricanes, wildfires, and floods have forced millions to relocate. The difference? American migrants often have insurance, legal protection, and media attention. The poor do not.

Climate change does not respect borders. But borders are being fortified in anticipation of climate flight—not to help, but to exclude. This is the great contradiction: the countries most responsible for emissions are erecting the highest barriers against their own consequences.

Colonial Echoes Still Resound

Migration patterns are not random. They trace the routes of empire.

France receives Algerians and Senegalese. The UK receives Pakistanis and Nigerians. Portugal, Brazilians and Angolans. These are not coincidences. They are consequences.

Colonialism extracted wealth, shattered institutions, and restructured economies for imperial convenience. When independence came, it often left behind weak states, fragile borders, and deep dependency.

Today's migration is frequently cast as reverse invasion. In reality, it is historical return: people following the flows of language, loss, and extraction that once came in the opposite direction.

Colonialism never fully ended. Its legacy lives in underdevelopment, and its infrastructure still guides the movement of people.

Inequality as System, Not Accident

Where you are born shapes everything: your lifespan, safety, income, and rights.

A doctor in Malawi may earn one-tenth of what a doctor in France earns. A garment worker in Bangladesh makes in a year what a Parisian makes in a week. These disparities are not simply about effort or skill. They are built into trade regimes, investment flows, and labor mobility controls.

In this system, people are told to stay put, while their labor value is exported.

Yet migrants are often criminalized. The Nigerian on a boat to Italy is labeled a smuggler. The Salvadoran crossing the Rio Grande is caged. The Filipino domestic worker in Hong Kong is forbidden from sitting in public parks.

Still, their remittances—over $800 billion in 2023—sustain entire economies. Migration is punished—but essential. Denied dignity—but demanded in practice.

This is the global economy's moral inversion.

The Unfree Market of Movement

Goods move freely. Data moves freely. Capital moves freely. But people?

People are told to stay—especially if they are poor, brown, or from the Global South.

Wealthy countries have designed migration regimes not to manage mobility—but to contain it. Visa restrictions, biometric scanning, offshore detention, airline fines. These do not end migration. They make it deadlier—and more profitable for smugglers.

Meanwhile, those same countries rely on migrant labor to pick fruit, build homes, clean hospitals, and care for children. Often undocumented. Often invisible.

This is not hypocrisy. It is intentional.

The system is designed to extract labor without offering rights. It wants the work, not the worker. The product, not the person. And it sustains itself through fear.

The Weaponization of Language

Migration is not just shaped by law. It is shaped by language.

In the 1930s, Jews fleeing Hitler were called "undesirables." In the 1990s, Rwandan genocide survivors were cast as a burden. Today, migrants from Yemen, Sudan, or Venezuela are framed as "floods," "hordes," "invaders."

These words are not descriptive. They are weapons. They turn trauma into threat, and survival into crime.

Media headlines focus on numbers, not causes. A child at a border becomes a legal challenge—not a moral one. A drowning family becomes a statistic—not a tragedy.

This is not accidental. It is how power shifts blame—from system to subject, from policy to person.

Migration as Human Truth

Migration is not a crisis. It is not a breakdown of order. It is what happens when systems fail and people refuse to die quietly.

It is not the problem. It is the response.

The real crisis is not movement. It is the conditions that make movement necessary: war, climate, inequality, and repression.

People move because the world moves beneath them. And no wall, no detention center, no border regime will stop the migration to come—unless we change the reasons people flee.

Migration is the world trying to breathe.

But while we argue about borders, we rarely ask a deeper question: when migrants arrive—who carries the weight?

The answer is not always what we expect.

It's time to re

Chapter 2 – Fortress Europe: The Politics of Deterrence and Denial

To much of the world, Europe once symbolized humanitarian conscience. The European Union, in its founding documents and postwar ethos, was imagined as a project beyond nationalism—a zone of law, dignity, and shared responsibility. It stood as proof that from the ashes of fascism, genocide, and colonialism, a new order could rise: moral, democratic, and principled.

That vision has collapsed.

Today, the European Union is not a refuge for the displaced. It is a fortress—militarized, externalized, and increasingly indifferent. Its policies are shaped not by legal obligation but political fear. Its borders have grown harder, its seas more dangerous, and its laws more cynical.

This chapter traces how Europe transformed itself from a defender of rights into a global laboratory of deterrence. It is not a story of capacity overwhelmed, but of values abandoned.

A Crisis of Reception, Not Volume

In 2015, over a million people—many fleeing the Syrian civil war—arrived at Europe's borders. The media called it a refugee crisis. But in truth, it was a crisis of reception. Europe, a continent of over 500 million people, was not overwhelmed by numbers. It was paralyzed by indecision and political fragmentation.

The EU's Dublin Regulation required asylum seekers to apply in the first country of entry. This meant that frontline states like Greece and Italy bore the brunt, while wealthier northern states could opt out. Attempts to create a fair distribution mechanism collapsed. Nationalism trumped solidarity. Germany opened its doors briefly—and paid a political price.

The real crisis was not logistical. It was moral. Europe failed not because it could not respond, but because it chose not to agree on what responsibility looked like.

Externalization: Cruelty by Proxy

Rather than fix its asylum system, Europe outsourced it.

In 2016, the EU struck a deal with Turkey: in exchange for billions in aid, Turkey would intercept asylum seekers and take back those who crossed into Europe. Similar arrangements followed with Libya, Tunisia, and Niger. The EU paid authoritarian or fragile states to act as gatekeepers—detaining, diverting, or deporting migrants before they reached European shores.

The consequences were brutal. In Libya, migrants were intercepted at sea and returned to detention centers rife with torture, rape, and forced labor. The EU funded and trained the very forces that committed these abuses. In effect, Europe shifted its legal obligations onto countries that would not honor them.

This was not a temporary fix. It became architecture.

Europe did not stop migration. It rerouted the suffering.

The Criminalization of Rescue

Under international maritime law, rescuing those in distress at sea is mandatory. Yet across the Mediterranean, humanitarian NGOs have been harassed, prosecuted, and blockaded.

Ships like Sea-Watch and Open Arms have saved thousands from drowning—only to face impoundment, legal threats, and smear campaigns. Volunteers have been accused of human smuggling. Captains have faced prison. Ports have been closed.

The message is chilling: not only are migrants unwelcome, but those who aid them are enemies of the state.

Europe has redefined the sea—not as a place of refuge, but as a weapon of deterrence. Empathy itself has become suspect.

Fortress Europe's New Walls

While the EU still lacks a coherent asylum framework, it has built a formidable border regime. Frontex, the EU's border agency, has seen its budget and mandate explode. It now deploys drones, ships, and surveillance systems across the Mediterranean and Balkans.

Frontex has been implicated in covering up illegal pushbacks—forced returns without due process—particularly in Greece, Croatia, and at the Polish-Belarusian border. Migrants have been beaten, robbed, and abandoned in forests or at sea. Investigations mount. Accountability does not.

Physical walls have followed. Greece fortified its land border with Turkey. Hungary sealed itself off. Poland erected a steel barrier against Belarus. Spain reinforced its North African enclaves with razor wire.

These are not temporary measures. They are permanent fortifications. Fortress Europe is no longer a metaphor. It is policy rendered in concrete and steel.

Fear as Currency

Across Europe, far-right parties have surged by turning migration into a political weapon. Viktor Orbán in Hungary warned of a Muslim invasion. Matteo Salvini in Italy criminalized rescue. Marine Le Pen in France built a movement on demographic fear.

But the fear has bled into the mainstream. Denmark's Social Democrats now support deportations to Rwanda. In the Netherlands, center-right coalitions endorse family separation. Even in Germany, the political center has shifted from integration to expulsion.

Migration has become a proxy—used to express fears about identity, economic change, and cultural loss. And migrants themselves have been turned into symbols—convenient targets in a broader crisis of European self-image.

Selective Compassion: Who Deserves Protection?

When Russia invaded Ukraine in 2022, millions of Ukrainians fled westward. Europe responded with speed and generosity. Temporary protection was granted. Schools and housing opened. Civil society mobilized. The response was humane and rapid.

But for Afghans, Sudanese, Syrians, and Somalis, the treatment was radically different. Brown and Black migrants faced detention, delay, and denial. African students fleeing Ukraine were blocked at borders. Asylum seekers from the global South continued to drown or be caged.

Europe showed what it could do—when it chose to. The disparity revealed a painful truth: compassion is not universal. It is selective, racialized, and political.

The Retreat from Responsibility

Europe did not face an invasion. It faced a test—and failed. It chose containment over compassion. It rewrote the rules it helped create. It turned humanitarian law into a performance of avoidance.

What makes this retreat so stark is that Europe helped design the very framework it now erodes. The 1951 Refugee Convention. The European Convention on Human Rights. The very ideals that once defined its postwar rebirth.

Today, those ideals are behind fences.

Migration will continue. So will displacement, war, and climate collapse. What remains in question is how Europe—and the world—chooses to respond.

Because the borders we build reflect not just our fears, but our values.

And the erosion of refuge is not just a European story.

It is a global warning.

Chapter 3 – The Walls We Build: Global Strategies of Exclusion

The story of migration today is not only about movement. It is about the lengths to which powerful nations will go to prevent it. Across continents, governments have invested billions in infrastructure, technology, and legal regimes designed not to welcome migrants, but to deter them—by any means necessary.

Migration is framed as a crisis. But the true crisis is political: a crisis of will, of policy, and of imagination. Instead of preparing for a more mobile future, many countries have chosen the path of denial. They build walls, delegate violence, and outsource moral responsibility. They invest in rejection—not reception.

These systems are not spontaneous. They are engineered. And they are global.

Europe's Fortress: Outsourcing the Border

In the wake of the Syrian civil war and other regional conflicts, Europe experienced what it called a "refugee crisis." But the deeper crisis was one of response. The European Union quickly began externalizing its borders—shifting enforcement to countries far beyond its own frontiers.

Deals were struck with Turkey, Libya, and other transit nations. In exchange for billions in aid, these governments agreed to block migration flows before they reached European soil. Libya's coast guard, trained and funded by the EU, has returned thousands of migrants to detention centers where torture, rape, and extortion are rampant. Turkey now hosts millions of Syrian refugees in limbo, unable to move forward and unwilling to return.

The Mediterranean became a graveyard. NGOs trying to rescue drowning migrants were criminalized. Fences rose in Hungary. Asylum laws were hardened. The message was clear: not here, not us.

Europe did not close its borders. It moved them.

The United States: Enforcement as Spectacle

The United States has long oscillated between its self-image as a nation of immigrants and its reality as an enforcer of exclusion. In recent decades, that tension has tilted sharply toward the latter.

The cornerstone of U.S. immigration enforcement has been deterrence through spectacle. Border walls. Militarized patrols. Family separations. Migrants—particularly from Latin America—are portrayed not as workers or refugees, but as threats to sovereignty.

Employer sanctions, first formalized under the Immigration Reform and Control Act of 1986, were intended to reduce undocumented employment. But in practice, enforcement focused on individuals, not businesses. Raids targeted workers, not exploiters. Punishment was selective—and racialized.

Under the Trump administration, cruelty became policy. Asylum seekers were forced to wait in Mexico under dangerous conditions. Children were caged. Refugee ceilings plummeted. While later administrations reversed some tactics, the underlying machinery of exclusion remains deeply intact.

What the U.S. perfected was a system that criminalized migration while depending on migrant labor. A contradiction sustained by silence and impunity.

Latin America: Exodus Without Destination

Migration in Latin America is shaped by two overlapping forces: structural inequality and state failure. Countries like Venezuela, El Salvador, Honduras, and Nicaragua have produced massive outflows of people fleeing violence, corruption, poverty, and political repression.

But few nations in the region have the infrastructure to absorb these migrants. Colombia has hosted millions of Venezuelans with little international support. Costa Rica and Panama face rising numbers of displaced people from Central America and beyond. The Darién Gap—once impassable jungle—is now a major corridor of desperation.

These migrants are caught in a net of indifference. Global north countries rarely offer resettlement. Border security is prioritized over protection. Human rights law exists on paper, but not in policy. Latin America has become both a source and a corridor of displacement, with few safe harbors.

Global South to Global Gatekeeper

A disturbing trend has taken root: wealthy nations increasingly pressure poorer ones to serve as gatekeepers. Whether through trade incentives, visa access, or outright payments, the Global South is being asked to do the Global North's dirty work.

Morocco patrols for Europe. Mexico detains for the United States. Niger monitors migrants for France. The logic is simple: keep migrants away from our borders, no matter the cost.

This is not burden-sharing. It is burden-shifting. It creates a world where asylum is a luxury for the geopolitically convenient, and where protection depends not on need—but on where you start your journey.

The Cost of Containment

The global containment system has produced more than just suffering. It has empowered cartels and smugglers. It has criminalized rescue. It has undermined international refugee law and dehumanized the displaced. And it has failed on its own terms.

People still move. They just do so in more dangerous ways. They climb higher walls. They cross harsher terrain. They trust more ruthless intermediaries.

What the world has built is not a migration system—but a deterrence regime. One that punishes the act of seeking safety, criminalizes hope, and rewards abandonment.

A Reckoning Ahead

This model is unsustainable. Climate change will displace millions. Demographic imbalances will grow. Conflict zones will expand. And the infrastructures of rejection—walls, camps, offshore prisons—will not hold back the tide.

The question is not whether people will keep moving.

The question is how we will respond when they do.

Do we build fences—or frameworks? Do we fund enforcement—or fairness? Do we respond to fear—or to fact?

Because in the end, the greatest border is not between nations.

It is between who we are—and who we dare to become.

Chapter 4 – The Asian Paradox: Dependency Without Acceptance

In the global conversation on migration, Asia stands as one of the most paradoxical and revealing landscapes. The continent is home to over half the world's population, the most dynamic economies, and some of the sharpest demographic transformations of the 21st century. And yet, it maintains some of the least open immigration systems on earth.

Across the region, countries send tens of millions of migrant workers abroad while simultaneously depending on imported labor to build cities, care for aging populations, and sustain economic growth. But the people who power these systems are often denied rights, settlement, or recognition. They are seen not as future residents but as disposable tools.

This is the Asian paradox: a profound contradiction between economic necessity and social rejection, between labor importation and legal invisibility. It is a model under strain—from aging populations, climate-driven displacement, and growing international scrutiny.

Japan: Demographic Collapse, Sealed Borders

Japan is aging faster than any other country. With a median age over 48 and a birthrate in decline, its population shrinks by hundreds of thousands each year. Rural towns are emptying. Care homes are chronically understaffed. Yet immigration remains a political taboo.

Despite growing need, Japan has kept its borders tight. Refugee recognition rates hover below 1%. Permanent immigration is discouraged. Even guest worker programs—branded as "technical trainees"—are designed to be temporary, limited, and largely restrictive.

These trainees often face long hours, poor conditions, and no path to citizenship. They cannot bring families. They cannot change employers freely. They cannot stay.

Cultural assimilation is considered nearly impossible. Foreigners are accepted only insofar as they remain invisible. But as Japan's economy quietly leans on foreign labor, this contradiction deepens—and becomes increasingly untenable.

South Korea: Behind the Smile, a Wall

Like Japan, South Korea faces demographic freefall. Its fertility rate is the lowest in the world. Seoul is a city of elders. And yet, despite labor shortages, South Korea has embraced immigration only reluctantly—and restrictively.

The Employment Permit System (EPS) recruits workers from Vietnam, Bangladesh, and the Philippines for industries like fishing and manufacturing. But it bars family reunification, limits job mobility, and offers no path to permanent residence. Migrants often live in segregated housing under surveillance, facing widespread discrimination—especially those with darker skin.

While Korean pop culture expands globally, its immigration debate remains provincial. The government knows it needs migrants. But it fears multiculturalism. That fear now shapes a society dependent on strangers it refuses to accept.

The Gulf States: Wealth Built on Stateless Labor

Few regions have developed faster than the Gulf Cooperation Council states—Saudi Arabia, the UAE, Qatar, and others. Their cities dazzle. But their growth has come through one of the world's most exploitative labor systems.

In many of these countries, migrant workers constitute the vast majority of the population. They build stadiums, staff kitchens, clean hotels, and care for children—yet remain legally voiceless, socially segregated, and perpetually temporary.

This is enforced through the kafala system, which ties a worker's legal status to a single employer. Migrants may have to surrender passports, endure dangerous conditions, and accept wages below subsistence. Changing jobs is difficult. Protesting abuse is often impossible.

Reforms have been announced—minimum wage laws, limited mobility—but implementation remains weak. Integration is not the goal. The prosperity of the Gulf has been built on exclusion.

Singapore and Malaysia: Efficiency Without Inclusion

Singapore presents itself as a model of global governance. Its migration system is carefully tiered: high-skilled talent is welcomed with incentives; low-wage laborers are imported under strict controls.

Migrant domestic workers from Indonesia and the Philippines cook and clean in affluent households. Bangladeshi and Burmese men work construction in tropical heat. But rights protections are minimal. Dormitories are overcrowded. Movement is restricted. Abuse is common and legal recourse rare.

Malaysia mirrors these trends, particularly in its plantations and factories. It draws heavily from South and Southeast Asian labor pools—but its enforcement systems are riddled with corruption, trafficking, and inconsistent oversight.

Both nations rely heavily on migration to sustain competitiveness. But neither extends inclusion. Migrants remain part of the machinery, not the society.

Refugees in Asia: The Missing Infrastructure

Asia also hosts millions of refugees—but without the legal or institutional frameworks to support them.

Bangladesh shelters nearly a million Rohingya Muslims fleeing genocide in Myanmar. They are confined to the massive, overcrowded camp at Cox's Bazar, lacking legal status or prospects for resettlement. Some have been moved to flood-prone islands against their will.

In Thailand, Myanmar refugees live in limbo. In India, Tibetans and Sri Lankans exist in ambiguous legal status. Most Asian nations are not signatories to the 1951 Refugee Convention, and regional coordination is minimal. Refugee policies are ad hoc, reactive, and deeply fragile.

Why the Paradox Persists

The roots of Asia's migration paradox are varied and entrenched.

National identities are often bound tightly to ethnicity, language, and cultural homogeneity. Historical trauma—from colonialism to civil war—fosters suspicion of the foreign. Many states maintain authoritarian or opaque governance structures that resist transparency and reform.

Public opinion is shaped more by silence and stereotype than open debate. Immigration is either ignored or framed as a threat to social harmony.

But at the heart lies a deeper truth: many Asian nations seek the benefits of migration—economic growth, labor supply, global relevance—without the responsibilities of inclusion. They want productivity without presence, movement without integration, labor without community.

That model is fraying.

Toward a New Social Contract

Asia cannot sustain its paradox much longer. The region's wealthiest nations are aging rapidly. Its labor needs are mounting. And its exclusionary models are increasingly at odds with global norms.

Migration has helped build Asia's prosperity. But prosperity without dignity is brittle. Economies built on invisible workers will fracture. Societies that refuse to include will eventually destabilize.

The Asian paradox is not destiny. It is a policy choice. And choices can change.

And then there is China—a superpower that rewrites the script entirely. It neither welcomes nor depends. Instead, it controls.

What does a migration-resistant superpower mean for a world in motion?

Chapter 5 – The China Exception: Control Without Dependence

For all its power, reach, and global entanglements, the People's Republic of China remains a glaring anomaly in the international migration landscape. It is not a magnet for immigrants. It resettles almost no refugees. It tightly regulates both inward arrivals and outward departures. Its citizens do migrate—by the tens of millions—but often under an unspoken condition: they remain tethered to the state, even abroad.

This is not a passive result of cultural inertia or bureaucratic backlog. It is strategic design.

Unlike the United States or the European Union, China has never anchored its national identity in immigration. Unlike the Gulf states, it does not rely on imported labor for domestic industries. Unlike India or the Philippines, it does not market itself as a labor-exporting country. Instead, China occupies a rare position in the global system: a superpower that engages the world economically while insulating itself demographically. It is a state that leverages global migration—but without welcoming it.

Hukou: The Internal Border

To understand China's migration model, one must begin within. Long before the world discussed border walls, China built one internally—the hukou system.

Established in the 1950s, the hukou household registration system ties a person's legal status, healthcare, education, and work rights to their place of birth. Originally designed to curb rural-to-urban migration, it has effectively created two strata of citizenship: urban insiders and rural outsiders.

As cities like Beijing and Shanghai ballooned during the economic booms of the 1990s and 2000s, rural migrants flooded urban centers to power construction sites, clean homes, and staff factories. They built China's prosperity—but were denied access to schools, social security, and voting rights. They were internal migrants without full recognition: the undocumented within their own nation.

Despite promises of reform, the Hukou system endures. It reflects a foundational truth in the Chinese governance model: movement must serve the state—not the individual.

Emigration as Strategy

China is not an immigrant nation—but it is an emigration superpower. More than 10 million Chinese citizens live abroad, as students, investors, laborers, and professionals.

But this migration is never disconnected from Beijing's interests. The Chinese state encourages outward movement only to the extent that it returns value. Scholars are lured back through state programs like the Thousand Talents Plan. Entrepreneurs are pressured to reinvest domestically. Political loyalty is expected, even from abroad.

Surveillance follows. Embassies maintain close ties with students and expatriates. Those who support dissident causes—like Hong Kong autonomy or Uyghur rights—may find their families in China threatened or their own passports canceled. Migration, here, is not liberation. It is strategic extension.

Belt and Road Labor: Export Without Integration

Through its Belt and Road Initiative, China has exported roads, railways, ports—and labor. Unlike Western firms that hire locally, Chinese state contractors often bring their own laborers to build foreign infrastructure.

These workers live in closed compounds, eat Chinese food, and rarely mix with host communities. Their presence is temporary, transactional, and tightly controlled. From Pakistan to Kenya, the resentment is growing. Local workers are excluded. Chinese compounds are fortified. The infrastructure may remain, but the relationships do not.

This labor model achieves maximum control with minimum cultural exchange. It globalizes Chinese presence without opening Chinese society.

Africans in China: Opportunity Without Belonging

In cities like Guangzhou, African traders, students, and entrepreneurs have built vibrant communities. But their reception is precarious.

Many face housing discrimination, visa harassment, and police targeting. During the COVID-19 outbreak, African residents were evicted from hotels, denied service at restaurants, and subjected to mass testing campaigns that carried echoes of apartheid. Officials denied racism. But the message was clear: China may allow temporary commerce—but not permanent belonging.

There is no path to permanent residency. No infrastructure for integration. No meaningful protection. It is migration without rights.

Refugees and Political Flight

Though China is a signatory to the 1951 Refugee Convention, its refugee system is nominal at best. The UNHCR operates under tight restrictions. Asylum claims are rare—and rarely granted.

Even internal displacement offers no protection. Uyghurs and Tibetans face constant surveillance, forced assimilation, and in many cases, detention. Those who flee abroad often face intimidation or repatriation efforts, with countries like Egypt and Thailand pressured to return Chinese dissidents.

In Hong Kong, protesters who sought asylum abroad were labeled traitors. Their families were harassed. Their documents revoked. In China's view, flight is not a cry for safety—it is an act of betrayal.

Surveillance Without Borders

Perhaps no other nation has exported domestic surveillance globally the way China has. From facial recognition tools to biometric archives, China's technology powers authoritarian regimes abroad—and monitors its own diaspora.

Chinese students abroad have reported being approached by consular "representatives," warned about political speech, or pressured to report on peers. Human Rights Watch has documented embassy-led harassment campaigns and threats to families back home.

Distance from China does not mean distance from its reach.

Why China Resists Immigration

China's aversion to immigration is not merely about economics. It is ideological.

The Chinese Communist Party promotes a model of national unity rooted in Han ethnic dominance and centralized authority. Ethnic minorities are tolerated—but only within tightly controlled bounds. Foreigners are guests, not potential citizens.

While facing demographic decline, an aging population, and shrinking labor force, China has shown little interest in immigration as a solution. Instead, it bets on automation, state-driven fertility programs, and internal retraining. It avoids the cultural complexities of integration, even at long-term economic cost.

This is not just policy. It is power preserved through homogeneity.

Migration Without Openness

China reshapes global trade, capital, and infrastructure—but resists becoming part of the global human commons. Its citizens travel but remain monitored. Its foreign workers build but are isolated. Its internal migrants labor but lack rights.

This is not an oversight. It is intentional architecture.

In a world where migration is redefining borders, economies, and identities, China's decision to wall itself off—legally, ideologically, and culturally—may prove one of the most consequential strategies of the 21st century.

Because across all systems and societies, one truth endures: the story we tell about migrants often matters more than the facts.

And the war over migration begins not at the border—but in the narrative.

Chapter 6 - Myths, Memes, and Morality: The War Over Migration Narratives

Migration is not merely about movement. It is about meaning—and meaning is often fought over relentlessly, strategically, and at times, deceptively. Before a migrant ever steps across a border, they are transformed into something else: a symbol, a threat, a victim, a burden, a hero, or a villain. Long before paperwork is filed or headlines are written, narratives are shaped. The terminology we use—"illegal alien," "economic migrant," "asylum seeker," "invasion," "dreamer," "queue jumper"—is far from neutral. These words are saturated with judgments, values, and political overtones.

This chapter explores the stories constructed around migrants—not those told by migrants themselves, but the ones imposed upon them. These stories are frequently false, sometimes cruel, yet always influential. We examine the myths that shape public perception, the memes that reduce complex lives to clickable content, and the morality plays that separate the "deserving" from the "undeserving." Ultimately, we must ask: who gains when migration is framed as a spectacle rather than as a human experience?

One prevailing myth is the metaphor of invasion. Phrases like "they are coming in waves" or "our country is being overrun" evoke images of chaos and threat. These are not neutral descriptors but fear-driven metaphors. Migrants are painted as floods, swarms, or tides—as if they are natural disasters rather than people. Though this rhetoric originates in far-right narratives, it has seeped into mainstream discourse. In reality, migration trends often contradict these alarmist portrayals. Net migration in the United States has at times declined or remained flat, even as anti-migrant rhetoric intensified. Europe saw a migration peak in 2015–2016, but numbers have fallen significantly since. Many of the countries crying that they are "full" are experiencing aging populations and labor shortages. The "flood" myth resonates because it stirs primal fears—territoriality, scarcity, xenophobia—but it is a narrative construction, not a demographic reality.

Another dominant narrative is the notion of a global "queue" for legal migration. Politicians often chastise migrants for "jumping the line," as if there exists a fair, orderly system in which everyone simply needs to wait their turn. But no such line exists. Instead, there are walls, lotteries, loopholes, and dead ends. Refugees frequently have no legal means to apply for asylum from within their home countries. Family reunification visas can take years—sometimes decades. Employment-based visas are tightly regulated by skill level, national origin, and quota systems. For many, there is no door to legality—only a wall. Desperation is not a matter of impatience; it is what remains when legality becomes unattainable.

Another trap is the binary between "good immigrants" and "bad immigrants." Public discourse often sorts migrants into two neat categories. The good ones are doctors, engineers, valedictorians, or veterans. The bad ones are criminals, benefit claimants, or unskilled laborers. This dichotomy, though convenient, is dangerously reductive. It implies that rights, safety, and dignity must be earned through exceptional productivity or assimilation. Most migrants, like most people, fall somewhere in between. They are learning, imperfect, ordinary—human. When we tie morality to economic contribution, we strip away humanity itself.

Today, migration narratives are increasingly shaped through social media. A single image can electrify or polarize millions. The photo of Alan Kurdi, the young Syrian boy washed ashore, ignited global grief. Footage of migrant caravans prompted militarized border responses. Surveillance videos are repurposed into fear-mongering political ads. Yet social media distorts reality: it erases context, simplifies complexity, and rewards virality over truth. Migrants are turned into content. Their lives become fodder for agendas—whether to inspire sympathy or incite anger. In both cases, their full humanity is lost.

The notion of moral worthiness still underpins asylum law. Refugees fleeing war are generally deemed "worthy" of protection, whereas those driven out by poverty, famine, or climate catastrophe often are not. This is a false and dangerous distinction, rooted less in principle than in prejudice.

Nowhere is this arbitrary line more glaring than in the plight of people displaced by climate change. The world is already witnessing a sharp rise in climate-related migration. Year after year, record-breaking floods, droughts, wildfires, and storms—intensified by global warming—force millions from their homes. Scientists warn that these numbers will surge in coming decades, possibly reaching tens of millions or more by mid-century.

Yet these uprooted families find little protection under today's rules. International refugee law was designed for those escaping persecution by other humans, not for people running from natural disasters. The 1951 Refugee Convention does not recognize "climate refugees" at all—there is no legal category for a farmer whose fields have turned to desert or an islander whose village has sunk beneath rising seas. So even if they cross a border seeking safety, they have no guarantee of asylum, no matter how uninhabitable their homeland has become. This legal void leaves climate-displaced people in limbo, unrecognized and largely unassisted.

Invisibility in the narrative compounds vulnerability on the ground. Having lost their homes to a crisis they did not create, climate migrants are often treated as if their suffering does not count. The injustice is stark: starvation and drought can be as lethal as bullets, yet those who flee such peril are told they have no right to safety. To suggest that a family fleeing famine or a sinking island is less deserving of refuge than one escaping a warzone is not legal reasoning, it is moral failure masquerading as law.

Control over migration narratives is wielded by a narrow few—politicians looking to shift blame, media networks chasing ratings, corporations shaping labor markets, and bureaucrats enforcing policy. Migrants rarely get to tell their own stories. When they do, their voices are edited, filtered, or boxed into predictable tropes: the grateful refugee, the tireless worker, the success story. Migrants who challenge the system, those who protest, organize, or demand justice—are often sidelined. In the realm of migration, controlling the narrative means wielding power. And rarely is that power in the hands of those who migrate.

The cost of false narratives is real. These are not just cultural tropes; they inform actual policies. They justify family separations at the U.S. border, offshore detention centers in Australia, pushbacks in the Mediterranean, and deportations into active conflict zones. Lies fuel cruelty, undermine international norms, and create moral numbness. Meanwhile, they distract from more fundamental questions: Why are people moving? What roles have receiving countries played in creating the conditions that cause displacement? What would a just, humane, and workable system look like?

If migration is the defining story of our time, then who tells that story matters deeply. To understand migration, we must reject frames that reduce it to a threat or a crisis. We must stop measuring migrants' "worthiness" and begin asking why societies are so eager to deny their worth. We must replace memes with memory, soundbites with testimony, and fear with principle.

This chapter has focused not on policy, but on perception. Yet perception shapes policy. Unless we reclaim the narrative of migration from those who distort it for gain, we will never forge a just future. Narratives shape belonging—and nowhere does that question strike deeper than in defining who is allowed to be part of a nation, and who is permanently excluded.

Migration is not just a disruption. It is a revelation—about inequality, about global interdependence, and about the resilience of people who refuse to accept the borders of injustice. To understand migration is to understand the world we have built—and to begin imagining one that is fairer, freer, and more humane.

Chapter 7 - Immigration and National Identity: Who Gets to Belong?

At its core, immigration is not merely about crossing borders. It is about entry into a national story—a shared narrative of identity, memory, and values. A nation is more than laws or geography; it is a living idea shaped by who is included, who is excluded, and who has the power to define "us." Immigration challenges this idea. It raises fundamental questions: Who gets to belong? Who has the right to participate in the story of the nation? And who decides?

This chapter explores the deep and often volatile relationship between migration and national identity. It examines how belonging is constructed—not just in legal terms, but emotionally, culturally, and historically. It shows how immigration stirs both hope and fear, and how it compels societies to confront the myths they live by. At its heart, this is a chapter about what it means to be part of a country that is unsure whether it wants to make room for anyone new.

While citizenship is often the legal marker of inclusion, it does not guarantee belonging. Across the globe, individuals who hold passports still struggle for acceptance. In France, children of North African descent may be citizens but are treated as permanent outsiders. In the United States, Asian or Latino Americans are frequently asked where they are "really from," despite generations of residence. A government can issue legal documents, but it cannot legislate social inclusion. Belonging comes not from paperwork, but from perception.

The way nations define identity often hinges on two principles: jus sanguinis (right of blood) and jus soli (right of soil). The former grants citizenship through ancestry, common in much of Europe and East Asia. The latter confers citizenship by birthplace, more typical in the Americas. But these principles are more than legal doctrines—they reveal cultural beliefs. Blood-based systems emphasize lineage and purity; soil-based systems emphasize participation and presence. Yet even countries that once prided themselves on inclusion are retreating. Germany tightened its nationality laws. The UK rolled back birthright rights. The U.S. regularly debates ending automatic citizenship for those born on its soil. These shifts reflect a deeper anxiety: that national identity is being rewritten by those deemed unworthy of the pen.

Race and religion remain some of the most entrenched barriers to belonging. In India, the rise of Hindu nationalism has cast suspicion on Muslims, even those with deep roots in the country. The 2019 Citizenship Amendment Act openly discriminated by granting fast-track citizenship to non-Muslim refugees, signaling a shift toward exclusion. In Israel, the nation-state law reaffirmed Jewish primacy, effectively relegating Arab citizens to a second-tier status. In Myanmar, the Rohingya were denied citizenship altogether—despite generations of residence—on the basis of ethnicity and faith. The result was not just exclusion, but statelessness and, eventually, genocide. These are not anomalies. They are part of a global trend in which identity becomes a gatekeeper, and immigration becomes a threat to be neutralized.

Language and cultural assimilation are often used as gatekeeping tools. Many countries require language proficiency for naturalization. But fluency doesn't always lead to acceptance. In Germany, children of Turkish immigrants may speak flawless German yet still face social and professional ceilings. French-Algerians may be fully integrated economically and linguistically but are still marked as "foreign." Assimilation is often treated as a moral test—but who decides when someone has assimilated enough? Is it the language they speak, the clothes they wear, the god they worship? The target is always moving, and the bar is rarely consistent. Even when migrants do "everything right," they may find that acceptance remains out of reach.

National identity is not fixed; it is forged through stories. Yet many of those stories are selective. Nations tell origin myths that emphasize unity and virtue, while downplaying conquest, exclusion, or complicity. The United States prides itself on being a nation of immigrants, even as it has enacted exclusionary policies from the Chinese Exclusion Act to the Muslim Ban. France upholds secularism, but bans headscarves in a way that disproportionately targets Muslim women. The United Kingdom celebrates diversity, but the Windrush scandal revealed just how conditional that celebration can be. Immigration reveals these contradictions. It shows that national identity is not only built—it is contested, negotiated, and often weaponized.

Populist leaders have weaponized identity politics to galvanize opposition to immigration. Hungarian Prime Minister Viktor Orbán warns of a threat to "Christian Europe." Donald Trump described migrants as criminals, invaders, and cultural contaminants. In France, Marine Le Pen paints a picture of a nation besieged by foreign influence. These narratives are potent because they manipulate legitimate feelings of fear and uncertainty. But they also draw false lines—reducing complex human beings to caricatures. They offer clarity at the expense of truth.

In these debates, the burden is usually placed on migrants to "integrate." Rarely is the same demand placed on the host society to make space. But belonging is a two-way street. It cannot be earned solely through adaptation. It must be reciprocated through recognition. A society that demands cultural conformity while offering no acceptance creates resentment rather than unity. Integration is not submission; it is participation. It means allowing people to contribute as they are, not only as others want them to be.

So, who gets to belong? The answer is not found in birth certificates or residency permits alone. It lies in a nation's willingness to expand its definition of "we." Nations that cling to an idea of identity as inheritance—a bloodline, a culture frozen in time—will struggle in an interconnected, mobile world. But those that understand identity as a conversation—as something that evolves through inclusion—will be better prepared to thrive.

Immigration is not only a demographic fact. It is a moral mirror. It forces us to ask not only who belongs, but who we are. True belonging cannot be bought or imposed. It must be offered. And it must be allowed.

Identity does not only exclude. It also enriches, adapts, and—at times—profits. Behind every wall and policy is not just fear, but industry. Migration has become business. And business, for better or worse, is booming.

Chapter 8 – The Business of Borders: Profit, Power, and the Industry of Exclusion

Borders today are no longer just geographical markers or symbols of national sovereignty. They have become markets—globalized zones of profit, reinforced by the logic of security and the currency of fear. What once was considered a matter of law and order is now a lucrative sector, sustained by a constellation of private contractors, defense corporations, data brokers, and political alliances. From high walls to high-tech scans, from detention centers to biometric tracking, the global apparatus of exclusion has expanded into a self-perpetuating economy—one where human mobility is treated not as a humanitarian concern, but as a security threat to be managed, monitored, and monetized.

The physical elements of border control—walls, fences, guard towers—are often presented as protective barriers. But for those who build and supply them, they are business opportunities. In the United States, companies like Boeing, Lockheed Martin, and General Dynamics have secured billions in contracts to deliver drones, surveillance towers, and integrated systems to patrol the southern border. In Europe, defense and aerospace firms such as Airbus and Thales profit handsomely from EU border agency Frontex's growing enforcement and surveillance budgets. In Israel, border technologies first developed along the Gaza barrier have become a thriving export industry, marketed to nations across Africa, Asia, and Latin America. Fortress-building is no longer just a domestic policy—it's a business model and a global brand.

The reach of this industry now spans continents. Canada, often seen as a progressive voice on immigration, has quietly expanded its border surveillance contracts. The Canada Border Services Agency (CBSA) has invested in predictive analytics, facial recognition, and AI-powered risk detection—often in collaboration with U.S. or Israeli security firms. Meanwhile, Mexico, under pressure from U.S. policy, has militarized its southern border with Guatemala, effectively turning itself into a buffer zone. Latin American governments increasingly serve as subcontractors in a hemispheric border enforcement regime, all under the umbrella of diplomacy, aid, or trade deals.

The machinery of exclusion does not end at the wall. Detention has become its own economy. Across the U.S., private prison companies like CoreCivic and GEO Group operate large networks of immigration detention centers, where profit rises with occupancy. These corporations are paid per detainee, per night—a financial model that rewards prolonged incarceration and aggressive enforcement. In Australia, offshore detention has been outsourced to private firms under contracts that obscure accountability and inflate costs. In the United Kingdom, companies contracted to manage detention centers have been implicated in scandals involving abuse, neglect, and profiteering. When incarceration becomes a revenue stream, the line between justice and exploitation collapses.

Technology has expanded the border's reach beyond the perimeter. Biometric databases now collect and store fingerprints, iris scans, and facial recognition data from millions of migrants, including asylum seekers and refugees. Artificial intelligence is being deployed to flag "deceptive" behavior during interviews, despite the absence of rigorous validation. Risk assessment algorithms, shrouded in opacity, sort individuals into threat categories with no clear basis. These tools are sold as neutral and efficient, but they often entrench bias and reduce people to predictive profiles. And the border no longer ends at the edge of a nation. Surveillance technologies follow migrants into cities, schools, and workplaces—normalizing a society of suspicion.

Humanitarian spaces are no longer immune to this logic. In refugee camps and migrant aid centers, biometric registration has become standard practice. UNHCR and other agencies now work with private tech firms to collect identity data, ostensibly to speed up aid delivery—but this data is increasingly shared with state actors and intelligence agencies. Refugees who came seeking protection find themselves cataloged, monitored, and profiled. The boundary between protection and policing is becoming difficult to distinguish. What began as a humanitarian gesture is increasingly governed by the protocols of national security.

The business of borders thrives on crisis. To sustain the expansion of this security economy, the threat must be constant, amplified, and unresolved. Politicians invoke specters of terrorism, human trafficking, and disease. Media outlets stoke panic with sensational metaphors: waves, swarms, invasions. Corporations respond with ready-made solutions: fortified enclosures, surveillance drones, armored vehicles, detention logistics. The more migration is presented as a perpetual emergency, the more license there is to expand contracts, suppress scrutiny, and erode civil liberties. A permanent state of exception becomes the norm—and business is good.

This interdependence between conflict and control creates a devastating cycle. The same companies that sell arms and fuel conflict later bid on contracts to manage the displaced. Defense contractors who profit from warfare turn around and market refugee monitoring systems. Human displacement becomes a two-stage revenue stream: first in destruction, then in containment. The arms-migration loop is not an accident of capitalism—it is one of its clearest mechanisms.

The influence of private interests is not limited to supply contracts—it extends to policymaking itself. In the U.S., companies invested in detention and enforcement have spent millions lobbying for stricter immigration laws. Many contracts even contain "bed quotas," mandating a minimum number of detainees regardless of actual need. Around the world, former military officers and government officials often sit on the boards of border firms, creating revolving doors between public power and private profit. This entanglement corrodes democratic accountability and prioritizes enforcement expansion over humane governance.

In this transaction, something vital is lost: humanity. When borders become markets, people become commodities. Children are counted like inventory. Families are separated to "send a message." Asylum claims are presumed fraudulent until proven otherwise. Border deaths are chalked up as unavoidable consequences. And when accountability is subcontracted, responsibility becomes diffuse. The deeper question—why people move, what we owe them, and how to respond ethically—is buried beneath spreadsheets and security briefings.

There is another way. True security cannot be outsourced, weaponized, or turned into a ledger. It is built on the rule of law that serves people, not profits. It depends on transparency in enforcement, and the courage to pursue alternatives that do not equate dignity with danger. Community-based models of accountability, alternatives to detention, and investments in addressing the root causes of displacement—conflict, climate crisis, and inequality—can replace coercion with compassion. Borders are not inherently cruel. But they are often made so by choice.

Migration will not cease. Nor will borders. But the question is whether they must be brutal to be effective, or whether a new model is possible—one that protects both people and principles.

When we commercialize exclusion, we erode the very values we claim to defend. Sovereignty does not require cruelty. Security does not require profit. The business of borders is booming. But so must our resolve to challenge it—because the price of doing nothing is not just economic. It is moral.

Chapter 9 – Selective Compassion: Who We Help, Who We Don't, and Why

Compassion is one of the most invoked concepts in the global discourse on migration. Politicians speak of "opening hearts," news anchors praise nations that "welcome the stranger," and humanitarian rhetoric surrounds refugee resettlement campaigns. Yet beneath this language lies a pattern—not random, and certainly not impartial. It is a pattern of selectivity: of determining who receives care, who is ignored, and under what conditions such moral concern is deemed appropriate.

This chapter confronts the uneasy reality that compassion in migration is neither consistent nor universally applied. It is shaped by race, religion, geopolitics, historical memory, and media optics. Certain groups are embraced swiftly and generously. Others, despite equal or greater need, are met with suspicion or indifference. This divergence is not grounded in ethical reasoning but in political convenience.

When Russia invaded Ukraine in 2022, the response from Western nations was strikingly swift and unified. Millions of Ukrainians were displaced, and borders across the European Union opened almost overnight. Housing was arranged, residency protections were granted, and civil society mobilized in a rare display of solidarity. It was, by many measures, compassion at its best—prompt, organized, and visibly humane.

Yet that same moment revealed the conditional boundaries of empathy. Black and brown migrants attempting to flee the same conflict reported racial discrimination. African students were pulled off buses. Indian nationals were blocked at checkpoints. Simultaneously, Middle Eastern and Central Asian asylum seekers—Syrians, Afghans, Iraqis—many of whom had already endured years of displacement, remained stuck in limbo or faced pushbacks at Europe's periphery. The humanitarian response to Ukrainians was real. But it was not universal. It exposed a hierarchy of human worth, where whiteness, proximity, and familiarity shaped the parameters of care.

The double standard is not limited to Europe. In the United States, the contrast between rhetoric and policy has been glaring. After decades of involvement in Iraq, Syria, and Afghanistan—wars that displaced tens of millions—the U.S. accepted fewer than 20,000 Syrian refugees during the peak of that nation's civil war. Iraqis who had worked for American forces as translators or contractors were bogged down by bureaucratic delays, despite facing threats to their lives. Afghan evacuees following the U.S. withdrawal in 2021 were similarly placed in legal limbo, stuck in a purgatory of temporary parole and uncertain futures.

Compassion in these cases is eclipsed by fear—fear of terrorism, of religious difference, of political fallout. It is also shadowed by guilt. To offer safe haven to those displaced by American military action would require a public reckoning with complicity. It is often easier to otherize than to redress, to turn away than to admit responsibility.

One of the starkest examples of selective compassion is seen in the treatment of climate-displaced people. Around the world, from the Pacific Islands to the Sahel, from South Asia to Central America, rising seas, droughts, and collapsing agriculture are forcing millions from their homes.

These individuals are widely acknowledged as victims—but they are not recognized in law. International refugee frameworks do not consider environmental collapse a legitimate basis for asylum. As a result, climate migrants become the most sympathetic yet unprotected group in the world. They receive headlines, but not visas. Recognition, but not refuge. Their suffering is lamented—but not legislated for.

The problem extends beyond categories of cause. It lies in the very way we define legitimacy. Refugees fleeing war or persecution are deemed "deserving." Economic migrants, even those fleeing grinding poverty or societal collapse, are portrayed as opportunists. Yet in practice, these distinctions are often blurred. Hunger can be the result of political instability. Fleeing economic ruin can be as desperate as fleeing violence. But the refugee/migrant binary persists—because it gives governments a moral alibi. It allows the semblance of compassion while preserving broad exclusion.

Media plays a decisive role in shaping these boundaries. The world mourned the image of Alan Kurdi, the Syrian toddler whose body washed ashore in 2015. That photo changed public sentiment—briefly. Similarly, images of Ukrainian mothers shielding their children in bomb shelters captured hearts and headlines. But many+96 crises go unfilmed. Refugees dying in the Sahel desert or drowning en route to Malaysia are barely noticed. When Haitian migrants crossed the Rio Grande in 2021, they were met not with empathy, but with mounted patrols and viral contempt.

Visibility governs compassion. What we see determines what we feel. And what we feel can decide who is helped—

and who is left to disappear. Selective compassion, in this sense, is a byproduct of selective storytelling.

Sometimes, compassion arises not from the present, but from the past. Historical responsibility has, in moments, opened borders. Britain took in Ugandan Asians expelled by Idi Amin. France accepted pieds-noirs and Algerian collaborators after independence. Germany's admission of over a million Syrian refugees in 2015 was widely interpreted as a moral gesture rooted in its 20th-century legacy. But even this impulse is inconsistent. Nations that have benefited from colonialism often resist aiding those displaced by its lingering consequences. When history is confronted, responsibility may follow. When history is denied, so is moral obligation.

Religion and racial identity further complicate the map of compassion. Across the West, Christian refugees from the Middle East are prioritized over their Muslim counterparts. In India, Hindu refugees receive expedited processing, while Muslims from similar backgrounds are detained or denied. These decisions are rarely about need. They reflect cultural affinity and political calculus. Compassion becomes less about vulnerability and more about compatibility with dominant identities.

What would it look like to create a truly principled ethic of protection—one that does not rely on race, religion, media coverage, or geopolitical alignment? Such an ethic would be blind to the optics of suffering and attentive to its reality. It would treat asylum not as a privilege for the visible, but as a right for the vulnerable. It would demand consistency—not just when compassion is convenient, but when it is uncomfortable.

True compassion is not reactive. It is not performative. It is not selective. It is built on the recognition of our shared humanity, across lines of faith, ethnicity, and origin. It challenges us to dismantle the unspoken hierarchy of whose lives matter most—and to replace it with a system that centers justice over convenience.

Much of this book has looked outward. But now, we turn the lens inward—toward the United States. Here, the crisis is not only one of migration. It is a crisis of truth: what we choose to see, what we choose to say, and whether we are ready to tell the full story.

Chapter 10 – America in Context: Myths, Hypocrisy, and the Manufactured Crisis

The United States does not face an immigration crisis. It faces a truth crisis—a crisis of narrative, of political will, and of moral clarity. The real emergency is not at the border, but in the stories the country tells itself: about who belongs, who benefits, and who to blame. Migrants are not the architects of chaos. That title belongs to elected officials, media empires, and corporate beneficiaries who manipulate migration not as a challenge to manage, but as a tool to distract, divide, and dominate.

This chapter seeks to strip away the myths that distort policy and the slogans that deflect accountability. It lays bare how immigration is used in the U.S. not merely as a domain of law but as a theater of fear—where the spectacle substitutes for substance, and where complexity is sacrificed on the altar of electoral optics. What America calls a "crisis" is not one of capacity, but of convenience; not of numbers, but of narratives.

Every election cycle, the U.S.-Mexico border is transformed into a stage. Politicians parade before cameras, flanked by barbed wire and border patrol agents. They promise crackdowns, sign executive orders, and posture with rhetorical bravado. But the reality behind these performances is far less dramatic—and far more nuanced. Border crossings rise and fall due to global instability, economic desperation, and seasonal movement, not domestic political cycles. he majority of undocumented immigrants in the U.S. didn't cross the southern border in a surge; they arrived legally—on visas—and overstayed. That quiet, bureaucratic reality rarely makes headlines, but it tells a far more important story about how immigration actually works.

This is not a failure of planning—it is a model that generates disorder by design. Manufactured dysfunction fuels political outrage and ensures a constant flow of headlines, campaign slogans, and budgetary justification for ever-harsher enforcement. The goal is not to solve the problem but to perpetuate it.

The system thrives on numbers, not justice. The more migrants are detained, the more the machinery is fed—regardless of whether those individuals pose any threat or have legitimate claims to stay. It is an economy of incarceration masked as national security.

The foundation of this system is a series of legal fictions—widely accepted yet fundamentally false. We pretend there is a line people can simply join to immigrate "the right way." No such line exists for most. We pretend asylum seekers can safely apply from their home countries. They cannot. We pretend people displaced by climate disaster are not refugees. Legally, they are not—but morally, they clearly are. We pretend Deferred Action for Childhood Arrivals (DACA) recipients are protected, yet they remain in limbo—granted temporary reprieve without permanent resolution, their lives suspended between political cycles and legal uncertainty.

The public is fed a distorted view of immigration. Polls show broad support for "legal immigration" and deep concern about "illegal immigration." But few Americans understand how few legal paths truly exist, or how seeking asylum is a legal right under international law. The gap between perception and policy is not accidental—it is cultivated. Politicians and media outlets deploy emotionally charged rhetoric, while the facts remain buried. The result is a population moved by sentiment, not substance.

"Illegality" becomes less about paperwork and more about appearance—about language, color, and cultural cues. Enforcement is not blind; it is guided by profiling, bias, and a long history of racialized exclusion.

The border, in this light, becomes not just a physical barrier—but a monument to historical amnesia. It is the outward expression of a national tendency to forget the contributions of migrants while memorializing the fears that justified their exclusion.

This pattern is not the failure of one party. It is a bipartisan abdication of moral leadership. Democrats talk inclusion, yet oversaw mass deportations under the Obama administration. Republicans fan border hysteria, even as they block reforms they once championed. The Biden administration rolled back many Trump-era restrictions, only to quietly reintroduce some under new labels. There is no moral high ground here—only political expediency and institutional cowardice.

Every broken policy leaves behind real human consequences. Children are separated from parents and lost in bureaucratic limbo. Asylum seekers are deported into violence. Longstanding residents with homes, families, and jobs are detained without warning. These are not the anomalies of a broken system. They are the intended outcomes of a system designed to punish rather than protect—to deter rather than understand.

Reform would shift the balance—empowering workers, disrupting profiteers, and removing the wedge issue politicians rely on. But until that happens, the incentives favor dysfunction over durability, fear over fairness.

In the end, the border is not just a line. It is a mirror. It reflects what America values, what it fears, and what it is willing to believe in order to preserve its myths. The chaos at the border is real—but it originates not in the movement of people, but in the manipulation of truth.

Until the United States confronts the gulf between its stated ideals and its actual policies—between its declared principles and its daily practices—the so-called crisis will persist. Not because of who comes, but because of who we have chosen to be.

The American debate is loud and often provincial. But migration is not an American anomaly. It is a global phenomenon. A rising tide that challenges every nation—and offers every society a choice: to resist change through fear, or to shape the future with courage and compassion.

Chapter 11 – The Global Tide: Migration in the 21st Century

Migration is not a wave. It is a tide. It rises and recedes, flows and crashes—but it never truly stops. In the 21st century, that tide is reshaping the planet, not as a temporary disruption, but as a permanent force. Human mobility is now driven by structural conditions—demographic shifts, climate collapse, deepening inequality, and political repression—that show no signs of reversing. Migration is no longer a side effect of crisis. It is the defining story of our global age.

The world continues to speak of "solving" or "stopping" migration, but these notions are illusions. The more urgent and honest questions are these: How will we manage the inevitable? Who will be protected, and who will be punished? Who will benefit from movement, and who will be left behind?

One of the clearest forces shaping the future of migration is demographic imbalance. In regions like Sub-Saharan Africa, population growth is accelerating. Many countries are expected to double or triple in size by mid-century. Meanwhile, in much of Europe and East Asia, fertility rates have plummeted, and populations are aging rapidly. Nations like Japan, South Korea, and Italy are facing the stark prospect of economic stagnation due to shrinking workforces and increasing dependency ratios.

These divergent trends generate natural migratory pressures—from younger, poorer regions to older, wealthier ones. But instead of planning for this reality, many receiving countries attempt to resist it. Borders are tightened. Immigration is restricted. And in doing so, the world heightens the very instability it fears. The need for labor, growth, and renewal persists, but the pathways to meet those needs are blocked.

Climate change has become a dominant engine of displacement. Rising seas, worsening droughts, crop failure, and extreme storms are rendering entire regions uninhabitable. In Bangladesh, encroaching seawater is threatening tens of millions. In the Sahel, expanding deserts are forcing pastoral communities off ancestral lands. Island nations like Tuvalu and Kiribati are watching their shorelines disappear. The UN projects that over 200 million people may be displaced by climate-related events by 2050.

Yet climate refugees do not exist in international law. There is no protection regime, no asylum process, no resettlement quota for those whose homes are erased by natural forces. They live in what might be called "displacement without recognition"—seen as victims in headlines but invisible in policy. They embody a contradiction: acknowledged as suffering, but denied rights. In a world heating beyond its political imagination, this legal void represents one of the gravest failures of the global system.

The economic forces behind migration are no less urgent. Globalization has created immense disparities in wealth and opportunity, both between and within nations. For many, migration is not ambition—it is survival. People flee collapsing economies, gang violence, state corruption, and hopelessness. Latin Americans journey north to escape inflation and insecurity. South Asians labor under contract in Gulf states, often under conditions of exploitation. Africans risk death crossing deserts and seas for the mere chance at stability. These are not reckless adventurers—they are rational actors responding to untenable conditions, making the only choice left to them when all others have been foreclosed.

And yet, receiving nations depend on this labor. Migrants pick the crops, clean the rooms, pour the concrete, and care for the aging. Their labor is essential—and systemically devalued. Migrants are treated as disposable inputs in a global labor market designed for extraction, not inclusion. What many countries call "immigration policy" is in fact a strategy of exploitation: accept the work, but deny the worker a path to dignity.

Political repression and authoritarianism continue to displace millions. The 21st century has seen the forced exodus of Syrians, Venezuelans, Afghans, Rohingya, and South Sudanese—among many others. Stateless minorities, dissidents, and persecuted communities face eradication with few options for refuge. Despite the presence of international asylum law, global protection systems are stretched thin and plagued by inequality. Some countries take in thousands. Others take in none. The right to asylum remains enshrined in law but endangered in practice—undermined by rising nationalism, shrinking humanitarian commitments, and a growing willingness to treat displaced people not as rights-holders, but as threats to be contained.

The global response to these pressures has been contradictory. Even as migration becomes more complex, the dominant reaction has been defensive. Walls are rising—figuratively and literally. Hungary built razor-wire fences to deter movement. India has fenced off its border with Bangladesh. The United States has fortified its southern frontier while expanding deportations and detentions. These barriers do not stop movement. They reroute it, make it deadlier, and enrich smugglers and traffickers.

But resistance is not the only response. Grassroots solidarity movements are emerging across the world. Migrant caravans from Central America are acts of mutual protection and defiance. Legal advocacy networks in Europe are winning victories against unjust detentions. Community sanctuaries are growing in North America. These movements remind us that while governments build borders, people build bridges.

The facts of migration are indisputable. But the deeper question remains moral: What does our response to migration say about us? Are we prepared to confront the causes of displacement? Are we willing to build systems that protect, rather than punish? Or will we continue to respond to the movement of people with the hardening of hearts?

Migration is not a crisis to be solved. It is a reality to be shaped. The future will be mobile—because the forces pushing people to move are structural, permanent, and global. The only real question is whether our politics, laws, and moral imagination will evolve to meet that future—or whether we will continue to deny it until denial becomes untenable.

The tide is rising. What we build in its path will determine more than borders. It will define who we are.

Chapter 12 – A Moral Reckoning: Who We Are When the Borders Close

Every civilization reaches a moment when its treatment of the outsider becomes more than a question of policy—it becomes a measure of its soul. For many nations, that moment is no longer in the future. It is now.

Migration is not a crisis. It is a test. A test not only of legal systems and national security protocols, but of collective memory, moral character, and our willingness to confront uncomfortable truths about ourselves. This chapter is not about numbers. It is not about border statistics, visa quotas, or asylum backlogs. It is about identity. Who we are. Who we pretend to be. And who we become when we turn our backs on others in need.

I. Historical Amnesia and the Fortress Illusion

The great irony of the modern migration debate is that many of the loudest voices calling for exclusion belong to nations built by migrants. The United States, Canada, Australia—each owes its existence to waves of voluntary and forced migration, from settlers and laborers to refugees and the enslaved. These countries were never hermetically sealed. They were shaped by motion, by displacement, by people arriving with nothing but survival in mind.

Yet today, these same nations posture as fortresses, acting as if their borders were carved into stone by divine decree. As if the idea of national purity were something more than a fragile invention.

This is not national security. It is historical amnesia. It forgets the Irish who fled famine, the Jews who fled pogroms, the Vietnamese who floated across oceans on wooden boats, the Haitians and Salvadorans who came from the rubble of U.S.-backed wars. It forgets that today's migrant is no different in desperation or dignity than those who came before.

II. The Language That Erases Humanity

The road to cruelty begins with language. Before borders are militarized, minds are primed. Migrants become "illegals," "invaders," "floods." These are not neutral terms. They are linguistic weapons—designed to strip away individuality, to erase stories, to make compassion feel optional.

When detention becomes "processing," when deportation becomes "removal," when barbed wire is described as "security infrastructure," we are not simplifying—we are anesthetizing. We are making violence palatable by naming it as policy. And the more abstract our language becomes, the easier it is to tolerate suffering.

This is not just a political tactic. It is a cultural failure. A failure to see migrants as fellow human beings rather than variables in someone else's ideological calculus.

III. The Moral Toll of Institutionalized Exclusion

The human cost of anti-migrant policies is often measured in body counts and economic loss. But there is another toll—quieter, deeper, and more corrosive: the erosion of moral clarity. What happens to a society that builds systems where compassion is treated as a loophole, and cruelty is codified as routine?

In some countries, teachers are told to report undocumented students. Doctors are instructed to verify immigration status before administering care. Employers quietly exploit migrant labor because the workers—trapped in illegality—cannot protest. These policies do not protect borders. They convert ordinary citizens into enforcers of fear. They turn care into surveillance, and everyday life into a theater of suspicion.

This is not just a loss of rights for the migrant. It is a loss of innocence for the host society.

IV. Conditional Humanity and the Politics of Worth

In moments of crisis, the hypocrisy becomes unmistakable. When war broke out in Ukraine, nations that had previously closed their doors to Syrian or Afghan refugees opened them widely for fleeing Europeans. Aid flowed. Visas were expedited. Social media campaigns surged with empathy.

But when Black or brown refugees arrive—whether from conflict, climate disaster, or economic collapse—they are met not with welcome, but with bureaucracy, detention, or silence.

This is not an argument against helping Ukrainians. It is a question about why that help is not universal. Why empathy is rationed by skin color, religion, or origin. And whether we are willing to admit that the humanitarian impulse is too often constrained by prejudice.

Humanity is not something that should have to be earned.

V. The Faith Traditions We Abandon at the Border

Nearly every major religion teaches a version of the same principle: welcome the stranger. Care for the traveler. Protect the vulnerable. The Torah commands it. The Gospels echo it. The Quran demands it. Hindu and Buddhist teachings affirm it.

And yet, as the world builds walls, detains children, and strips rights from the displaced, these moral teachings are not rejected outright. They are simply ignored. They become ritual words spoken on sacred days, detached from practice. Their call to conscience is buried under national interest.

We do not suffer from a lack of moral instruction. We suffer from selective obedience.

VI. The Reckoning That Awaits

There will come a time—sooner than we think—when the generations now in power will be asked what they allowed. What did we do while desperate people froze in border zones? While children were separated from parents in the name of deterrence? While camps overflowed and bureaucracies stalled, and silence was purchased with convenience?

We will not be remembered for our talking points. We will be remembered for what we permitted.

Silence, too, is a decision. And moral clarity delayed is moral clarity denied.

VII. Writing the Final Lines of This Era

The global migration story is not ending. It is only beginning. But the chapter we are writing now—how we respond to the stranger, the refugee, the person fleeing unlivable circumstances—will be remembered as either a triumph of principle or a collapse into fear.

We face a choice. Not as liberals or conservatives. Not as nations or governments. But as people.

To be defined by borders—or by bridges.

To be remembered for our silence—or for our courage.

To write a record of exclusion—or of radical, principled welcome.

The world is watching. So are our children. And the judgment will not be based on how high our walls were, but how deeply we remembered who we were supposed to be.

Chapter 13 – The Future in Motion: Migration in a Shifting World

There is no final word on human migration. It is as enduring as hunger, as elemental as birth, as political as war. But the patterns now emerging—driven by climate collapse, demographic imbalance, and political hardening—are unlike anything the modern world has ever witnessed. What we face in the coming decades will test every institution built to manage human movement, and every moral claim made about fairness, justice, and belonging.

This is not a forecast. It is a reckoning. The future of migration will not be defined solely by numbers or borders. It will be defined by how we respond.

Will we evolve our systems—or escalate our cruelty? Will we build bridges—or bunkers? Will we prepare, or will we punish?

The answers are not yet written. But the questions are already upon us.

One of the most urgent challenges is the growing climate exodus. Climate change is no longer a distant threat. It is a present displacement machine. Rising seas are swallowing homes from Bangladesh to the Marshall Islands. Droughts are driving farmers from Central America, Ethiopia, and Syria. Cyclones and flooding have uprooted millions across South and Southeast Asia. The World Bank estimates over 216 million people may become internal climate migrants by 2050— and that figure does not include those who will be forced to cross borders in search of safety. These individuals have no formal legal status as refugees, despite being displaced by forces beyond their control. The world's legal frameworks have not caught up with the environmental realities reshaping human movement.

Yet international law has not caught up. Climate refugees do not exist in the legal sense. There is no binding protection regime for people displaced by environmental collapse. These migrants fall through the cracks: neither eligible for asylum nor compensated by climate finance. Their invisibility is not accidental—it is designed by a global framework more concerned with emissions targets than human fallout. What happens when the land itself turns against its people, and the law offers no refuge?

Demographics present another irreversible shift. Many of the world's richest nations are aging rapidly. Japan's median age now exceeds 48. Europe faces shrinking labor forces. The United States is quietly approaching shortages in healthcare, construction, and education. At the same time, Africa's population is expected to double by 2050, and South Asia's youth bulge remains massive.

Migration is not merely a challenge under these conditions—it is a solution. It is one of the only mechanisms capable of balancing demographic disparity. Yet instead of building policies to match this reality, many countries double down on fear. Political campaigns stoke racial anxiety. Media narratives portray migrants as threats. And short-termism blocks long-term planning. The result is a cruel paradox: societies that need migrants to survive are the ones most determined to exclude them.

In many parts of the world, migration is now unfolding under the shadow of authoritarianism. Strongmen and ruling parties have found in migration a reliable scapegoat. In Hungary, Viktor Orbán invokes a civilizational struggle against immigrants to justify illiberal governance. In India, the Citizenship Amendment Act has been used to marginalize Muslims. In the United States, the Trump administration rebranded cruelty as deterrence—caging children, banning travel, and celebrating deportations as political victories.

Across these contexts, migrants become tools in a broader authoritarian playbook: dehumanize the outsider, rally the base, and erode democratic norms under the guise of national security. Authoritarian leaders do not fear migration. They exploit it. They use it to concentrate power, erode pluralism, and delegitimize dissent. In this sense, immigration policy is no longer a separate domain. It is democracy policy. To defend the rights of migrants is to defend the rule of law itself.

Layered atop these political shifts is a technological transformation of border control. The future of exclusion is automated. Predictive analytics determine who is flagged as a "risk." Artificial intelligence monitors social media for ideological suspicion. Drones patrol deserts. Satellites scan coastlines. Biometric databases store fingerprints, iris scans, and facial recognition profiles for generations. All of it is sold in the language of "efficiency." But its true function is to make exclusion faster, quieter, and less accountable—to strip away the human face of enforcement and replace it with an algorithm. This digital wall may be invisible, but it is no less impenetrable, and far harder to question.

Automated borders do not reduce harm. They conceal it. They obscure accountability. And they create a world where rejection is instant, invisible, and unappealable. A future of high-tech walls is not more humane. It is simply more abstract in its brutality.

And yet, there is another way. The future is not written in code or concrete. It is shaped by the decisions we make now. Legally binding compacts on climate and migration can create shared responsibility and real protection. Regularized migration programs can meet labor demands while safeguarding human dignity. Humanitarian pathways can be designed to respond to displacement before it turns catastrophic. These are not hypotheticals. They are choices we are already making.

The lines we draw today—on maps, in laws, in policy—will shape the world to come. Will they be lines of division, or of duty? That is the question migration puts before us—not as a test of policy, but as a test of character.

The future is in motion. So must we be.

Conclusion – Lines We Draw, Futures We Choose

Immigration is not a crisis. It is a condition of life. From the first humans who walked out of Africa to today's asylum seekers at razor-wired borders, human movement has never ceased. What changes—what always changes—is how we respond.

This book is not a manifesto for open borders, nor a blanket defense of amnesty. It is a mirror and a map. A mirror to reflect the fears, distortions, and hypocrisies embedded in our institutions. And a map pointing toward a more honest, just, and sustainable path.

We have traced how borders have become industries, how compassion is rationed by race and narrative, and how the language of "crisis" is often a political invention. We have seen that the same nations that criminalize migration also depend on it economically. That displacement is driven by climate, conflict, and inequality—and that surveillance, not sanctuary, is the tool most often deployed in response.

We've examined how law is bent by power, how facts are buried beneath slogans, and how the global system increasingly rewards walls over welcome. We've named the hypocrisy: in America, where a nation of immigrants turns its back on the next; in Europe, where the spirit of Geneva now funds detention camps; in Australia, where asylum seekers are banished to remote islands.

This hypocrisy is not rhetorical. It is structural. It is sustained by a deep refusal to confront historical responsibility and contemporary complicity.

But this book is not about condemnation. It is about clarity. And clarity demands we ask not whether people will move—they will—but whether we will meet that movement with fear or foresight, with panic or principle.

We are entering an age of upheaval—of heat and hunger, war and water, labor and longing. The systems we build now will determine whether migration becomes a source of division or a platform for global cooperation. We cannot stop human movement. But we can shape it. Fairly. Humanely. Strategically.

This will require truth: public education that challenges lies, leaders who resist the pull of scapegoating, and citizens who ask more of the systems done in their name.

This will require law: international protections that recognize climate displacement, humane asylum frameworks, and labor mobility schemes that balance national needs with human rights.

And above all, this will require courage. The courage to tell hard truths, to see migrants not as threats but as reflections—of what we fear, of what we hope, of who we once were and may yet become.

We are not spectators in this story. We are its authors. The lines we draw—on maps, in law, in culture—will shape the world to come. They will decide whether we build corridors or cages, systems of fairness or fortresses of fear.

This is not a question of charity. It is a question of strategy. Of vision. Of moral imagination.

To leaders: Stop using migration as a weapon to win elections. Stop pretending that complexity justifies cruelty.

To citizens: Look harder. Ask more. The slogans are simple because the systems are not.

To those in motion: You are not alone. Your journey is not a crime. It is the oldest human instinct—the search for a better life.

Imagine a world where movement is not criminalized but managed. Where refuge is not rationed but respected. Where the laws we build serve dignity, not deterrence.

That world is still possible. But it is not promised. It must be chosen—and built.

Because in the end, the border is not where the world ends.

It is where the future begins.

References and Bibliography

Books & Monographs

- Anderson, Benedict. *Imagined Communities: Reflections on the Origin and Spread of Nationalism*. Verso, 1983.
- Arendt, Hannah. *The Origins of Totalitarianism*. Harcourt, 1951.
- Carens, Joseph H. *The Ethics of Immigration*. Oxford University Press, 2013.
- Collier, Paul. *Exodus: How Migration Is Changing Our World*. Oxford University Press, 2013.
- Fukuyama, Francis. *Identity: The Demand for Dignity and the Politics of Resentment*. Farrar, Straus and Giroux, 2018.
- Huntington, Samuel P. *Who Are We? The Challenges to America's National Identity*. Simon & Schuster, 2004.
- King, Desmond. *Making Americans: Immigration, Race, and the Origins of the Diverse Democracy*. Harvard University Press, 2000.
- Sassen, Saskia. *Guests and Aliens*. New Press, 1999.
- Shachar, Ayelet. *The Birthright Lottery: Citizenship and Global Inequality*. Harvard University Press, 2009.

Academic Journal Articles

- Carens, Joseph H. "Aliens and Citizens: The Case for Open Borders." *The Review of Politics*, vol. 49, no. 2, 1987, pp. 251–273.
- Walzer, Michael. "The Distribution of Membership." In *Boundaries: National Autonomy and Its Limits*, ed.

Peter G. Brown and Henry Shue. Rowman & Littlefield, 1981.

Reports & White Papers

- United Nations High Commissioner for Refugees (UNHCR). *Global Trends: Forced Displacement in 2023*.
- World Bank. *Migration and Development Brief 36: Migration and Remittances – Recent Developments and Outlook*, May 2022.
- International Organization for Migration (IOM). *World Migration Report 2022*.
- Pew Research Center. *U.S. Immigration Trends*, 2022.

News & Media Sources

- The Wall Street Journal – editorial coverage on immigration economics and policy.
- The New York Times – immigration case studies and global refugee crises.
- BBC News – coverage of EU migration policy and Mediterranean crossings.
- Al Jazeera English – investigative reports on global refugee flows.

Legal & Government Documents

- U.S. Immigration and Nationality Act of 1965 (Hart–Celler Act).
- U.S. Immigration Reform and Control Act of 1986.
- U.S. Department of Homeland Security, annual immigration enforcement statistics.

- Geneva Convention Relating to the Status of Refugees, 1951.
- European Union Dublin III Regulation.
- Canada's Express Entry immigration system documentation.
- UK Home Office: Points-Based Immigration System White Paper (2020).

Web Resources

- Migration Policy Institute – https://www.migrationpolicy.org
- UNHCR Statistics Database – https://www.unhcr.org/statistics
- U.S. Citizenship and Immigration Services – https://www.uscis.gov
- CIA World Factbook – https://www.cia.gov/the-world-factbook/

About the Author

Jonathan P. Saunders, MFA, LLM, is a former special warfare unit leader, international lawyer, and cross-border strategist with deep experience in high-risk and politically sensitive environments. He has advised both private sector clients and sovereign governments on international law, conflict response, and complex regulatory challenges.

Saunders is the founder of Saunders Consigliere PLLC, a firm licensed by the U.S. Department of Justice (DOJ) to represent immigrants—both documented and undocumented—in any U.S. immigration court. The firm also holds similar standing in the United Kingdom, allowing representation before British immigration authorities. While much of its work involves corporate clients with global labor footprints, Saunders remains personally involved in cases where immigration, sovereignty, and human dignity intersect.

This global, hands-on perspective shapes his writing. He approaches immigration not just as a legal problem, but as a human and geopolitical reality. In *Immigration: The Line We Draw*, he brings years of direct and institutional experience to bear on one of the most defining and divisive issues of our time.

A graduate of Indiana University, Saunders blends operational clarity with legal insight—writing from the belief that the systems we build to regulate movement often reveal more about power, fear, and identity than we realize.

www.ingramcontent.com/pod-product-compliance
Lightning Source LLC
Chambersburg PA
CBHW020559030426
42337CB00013B/1148